Sports Stars

CAROL JOHNSTON

The One-armed Gymnast

By Pete Donovan

◐ CHILDRENS PRESS, CHICAGO

Cover photograph: Mitchell Rose
Inside photographs courtesy of the following:
Carol Johnston, pages 13, 16, 25, 35, 37, and 41;
Lynn Rogers, pages 21, 29, and 39; David Hopley,
pages 6, 9, 11, 18, 23, 31, and 33.

Library of Congress Cataloging in Publication Data

Donovan, Pete.
 Carol Johnston, the one-armed gymnast.

 (Sport stars)
 Summary: A biography of the Canadian gymnast who won All-American honors in 1978 despite her physical handicap.
 1. Johnston, Carol, 1958- — Juvenile literature. 2. Gymnasts — Canada — Biography — Juvenile literature. 3. Physically handicapped — Canada - Biography — Juvenile literature.
 [1. Johnston, Carol, 1958- . 2. Gymnasts. 3. Physically handicapped] I. Title.
 II. Series.
 GV460.2.J63D66   796.4'1'0924   [B]   [92]   82-4449
 ISBN 0-516-04323-4   AACR2

Copyright © 1982 by Regensteiner Publishing Enterprises, Inc.
All rights reserved. Published simultaneously in Canada.
Printed in the United States of America.

 3 4 5 6 7 8 9 10 11 12 R 90 89 88 87 86 85 84 83

Sports Stars

CAROL JOHNSTON

The One-armed Gymnast

Carol Johnston was nervous. She stood at the end of the balance beam. She was waiting for her turn in the national gymnastics championships. "The beam looked like a mile long. But I knew it was only 16 feet," Carol remembers.

It was in May of 1978 in Seattle, Washington. Carol, who has only one arm, was one of the best gymnasts in the country. Now it was her turn on the beam. She would have to do very difficult moves on the beam. The beam is only four inches wide.

"I didn't do very well when I warmed up. I was so nervous," Carol says. Then suddenly her name was called. "I was eating chocolate ice cream and was almost late," she laughs.

Carol walked to the beam. It is almost as tall as she is. "I pretended it was just like practice," she says. "I had done 10 routines a day on the beam for three months. So I said to myself it wouldn't be that hard to do one more."

Everyone who had gone before Carol had fallen off the beam. She started with leaps in the air. She didn't fall. Then she did an aerial walkover, a flip with no hands. It was the hardest part of her routine. And she did it perfectly.

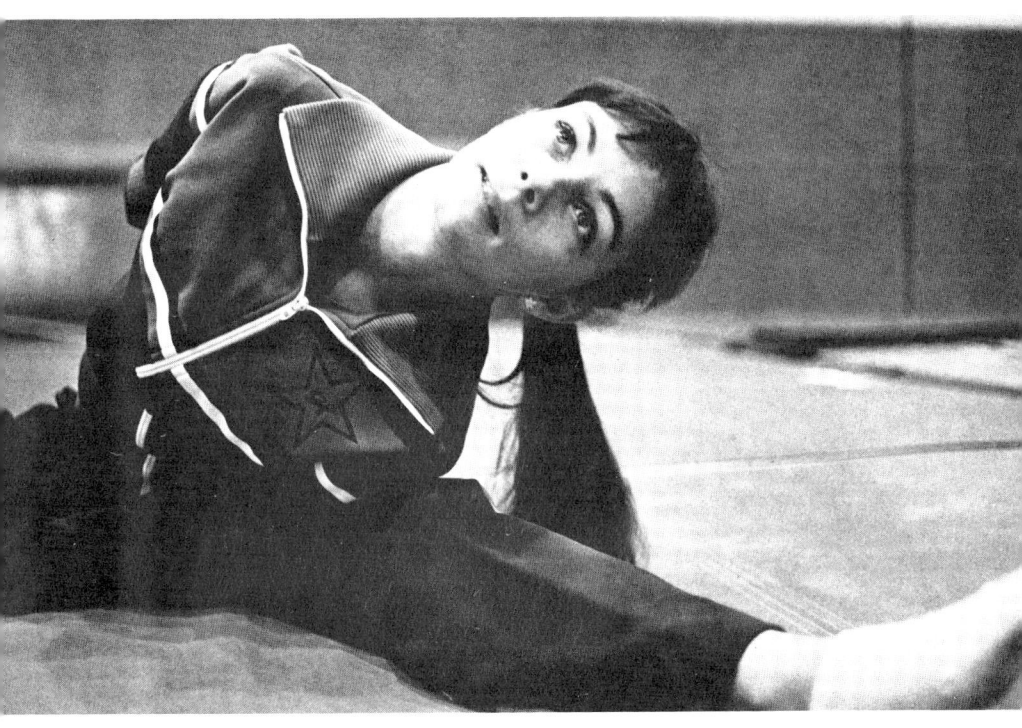

All athletes must warm up before they perform. Stretching exercises help Carol become limber.

Then it came time for her dismount. Carol went all out for it. She flipped off the beam. "I couldn't believe it," she said. "It was the best routine I had ever done. I felt good about what I had done even before I heard my score."

When Carol finished, her teammates all hugged her. Everyone in the audience clapped. Her score was 9.5 (a 10 is perfect). Only one girl in the United States had a higher score than Carol.

Carol was second. She was named an All-American.

Later that same day, Carol was the last performer on the floor exercise. She had to do dancing and tumbling routines.

Carol works on the uneven parallel bars. She switches back and forth and is always moving.

"I was really scared and nervous again," she said. "But the crowd was pulling for me. I tried to play to the audience. I waved and smiled at them."

Carol began performing on the floor. Everyone stood up and started to clap. She got a 9.6 score. She was All-American again.

These things were remarkable for anyone. But they were even more special for Carol.

Carol was born with only one arm. She never acted as if it were a handicap. Carol practiced hard. She believed she could do what she wanted. She proved she could.

A balance beam is 4 inches wide and 16 feet long. A gymnast tries to use the full length of the beam. She does jumps, leaps, running steps, and turns. Some good gymnasts do cartwheels, back handsprings, and somersaults. Here Carol performs in the Canadian Winter Games at Alberta in 1975.

Gymnastics is one of the hardest sports of all. You must be strong. You must be able to jump in the air, flip over, and land on your feet. Many people with two arms can't do gymnastics. But Carol can do almost anything.

She flips on the beam, which is dangerous. Carol can even do a double flip on the floor. She also learned to do moves on the bars and catch herself with just one arm.

Carol went to college in Fullerton, California at Cal State-Fullerton. Her friends called her "lefty." And a television movie was once made about her. Carol is small. She is 4 feet, 10 inches tall. She weighs just 83 pounds.

"I'm not supposed to be a gymnast physically," Carol said. "But no one told me that mentally. No one said I couldn't be creative with one arm."

So Carol became a famous gymnast.

She came to Cal State-Fullerton in 1976. She was 18 years old. Carol lived in Calgary, Canada, where it was very cold. The coach at Fullerton, Lynn Rogers, asked her to come to California after high school. Carol said yes.

"I thought I could improve as a gymnast at Fullerton," Carol said. "I also thought it would be good for me to be out on my own.

"I wanted to be challenged more as a gymnast than I was in Canada," she said.

To become a good gymnast, many hours must be spent practicing.

One of her teammates at Fullerton was Karilyn Burdick.

"Nobody believed she could do much. When she first got to Fullerton, all she could do was the basics," Karilyn said.

"She learned more than anyone there. She was totally unbelievable. Carol created a lot of excitement in the gym. We'd all look at her and say 'Wow.'

"She made all of us try harder because we saw what she could do with one arm," said Karilyn.

Coach Rogers wasn't sure how good Carol could be.

"I didn't know what her impact would be on our program," he said. "I thought she would help us. I thought she'd be a star because of her handicap.

"But she became a star based just on her gymnastic ability. Stars have something special inside them and Carol has that," coach Rogers said.

In her first year at Fullerton (1976-1977), Carol worked mostly with assistant coaches. Coach Rogers worked with the more advanced gymnasts.

"He didn't expect me to do really well," Carol said. "Maybe he just wanted to write a thesis on a one-armed gymnast," she laughs.

But Carol began to improve. She became the conference beam champion. She almost made it to the national finals. And she was still only a freshman.

Carol started to get a lot of attention from newspaper reporters and television announcers.

"I was a very quiet and shy girl in high school. I wanted to change that in college. All the attention I was getting sort of helped me do that.

"Everyone knew I was a one-armed gymnast. So I didn't have to be afraid or awkward about the fact that I had only one arm," she said.

"Before, I used to get a little upset. People were afraid to ask me about having only one arm.

But I always told people it didn't bother me. It didn't hinder me in any way.

"But I still wanted to be treated as a gymnast, not as a one-armed gymnast," Carol said.

The next summer, Carol stayed in Fullerton. She worked out. Some days she would practice six hours. She only took a day off once in a while.

"Most kids will learn one major move in gymnastics each year," coach Rogers said. "But Carol learned three that year — a back flip on the beam, a full cartwheel dismount from the beam, and an aerial walkover.

"She didn't have a high degree of difficulty in

her routines when she was a freshman. But she did by her sophomore year," he said.

Carol won the conference championships in both the beam and the floor exercise that year. Then she and her teammates went to the college national championships in Seattle, Washington.

"We knew what Carol could do. But I don't think anyone else in the country did," coach Rogers said.

Competing against the top college gymnasts from all over the United States, Carol was terrific.

"When she scored a 9.5 on the balance beam the crowd went crazy," coach Rogers said. "You

In the Western Canadian Summer Games in 1975 Carol tore the ligaments in her ankle on her first event on the uneven bars.

knew she was doing well during her routine. And a lot of our girls were crying.

"They were crying because they were so happy for Carol. I remember just standing there and hardly being able to believe what she had done," said coach Rogers.

"And then Carol did it again on the floor exercise," he said. "Those were two dynamite performances."

Coach Rogers knew how hard it was for Carol. "One thing you use your hands and arms for is to save a mistake. If you start to fall, you can brace yourself with your hands. Carol only had the one arm.

"And the other girls could get twice as much push with their arms. But Carol always had a dream and an ability to see things in her head."

That was one thing that made Carol special. She saw pictures in her mind of herself doing gymnastics. Then when she did them, she knew what she was doing.

"When we're kids we visualize all the time," Carol says. "We make things up in our head. Then when we get older everything is more logical. But because I had one arm I always had to be creative in what I did. Even something like tying my shoe I had to do differently."

One time Carol hurt her wrist. She couldn't

practice for two weeks. She had just done her first double backflip, the hardest trick in gymnastics she could do.

The first day Carol came back to practice, coach Rogers asked her what she wanted to work on. Carol said she wanted to try her double flip. "I've been practicing in my head for two weeks," she said. Carol did it perfectly. Then she did it perfectly again. "I think that shows the power of the mind," Carol said.

Another time, coach Rogers didn't think Carol could do a move on the bars. So he bet her a sweatsuit. Carol made it. The coach had to give her a new sweatsuit.

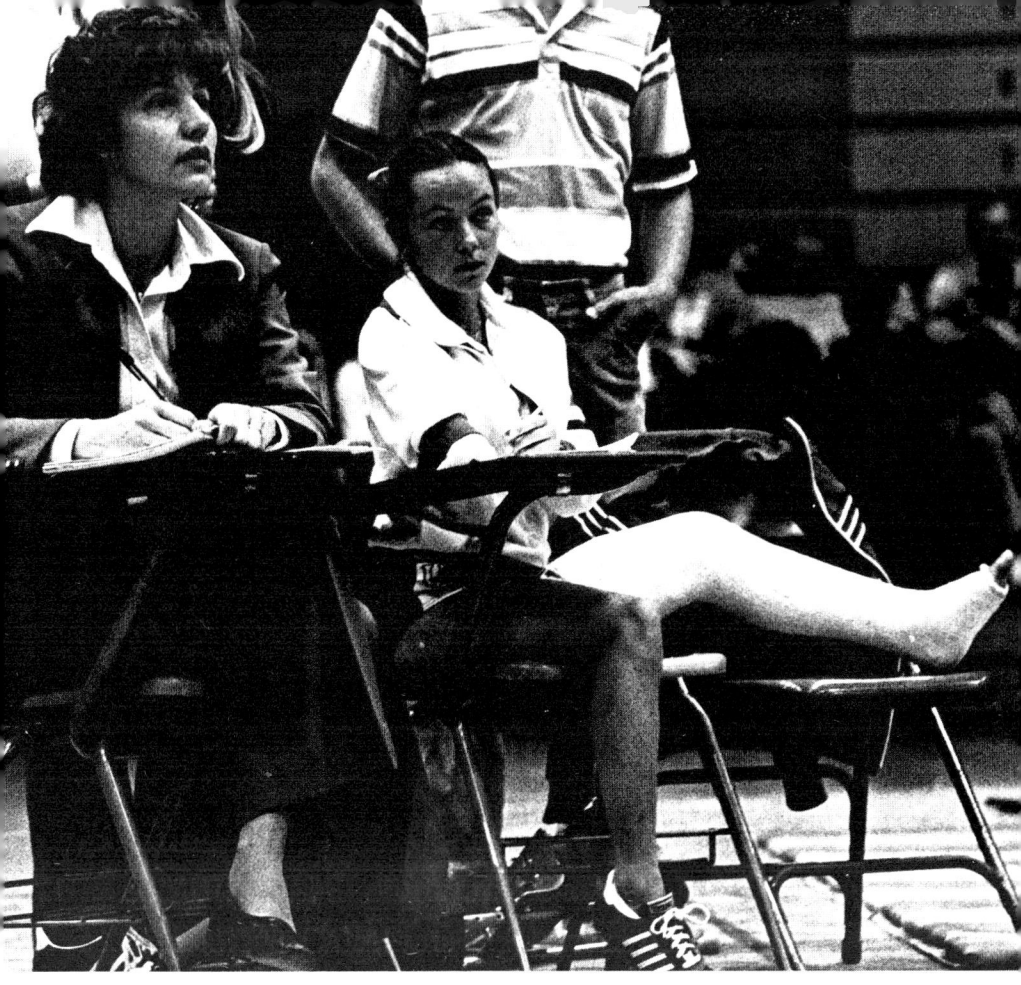

Less than a year after she won All-America honors in Seattle, Carol suffered a bad injury to her left knee. It happened in practice. She had to have an operation. She wore a cast for several months.

"Before I hurt my knee, gymnastics was my whole life," Carol said. "Then I had a chance to look at everything away from gymnastics. I knew something was missing."

So Carol made a comeback. She ran a lot when her cast came off. She worked extra hard in the gym.

"I knew what I wanted to do. I was intense in my training. I had a glimpse of what my life would be without gymnastics. I wasn't ready to give it up.

"Everyone was a little worried about my coming back, my coaches, my doctor. I was probably the most worried."

Balance is very important when working on the beam.

But Carol did make it back on the team. She competed again and helped her teammates win.

Then she hurt her knee a second time. The doctor operated and Carol faced a decision.

"The doctor told me I could make the knee strong enough to do gymnastics again," Carol said. "But if I ever injured it again, I might not be able to walk normally. So I decided to retire. It was time to lead a normal life.

"Having one arm was never a limitation, but my knee was," Carol said.

Carol was born in Calgary, Canada on March 10, 1958. Her sister, Judy, is three years older than Carol.

Although practice is important, Carol still had to study and do research in the library.

Carol's father, Walter Johnston, is a chiropractor. Her mother, Inez, is a housewife.

"The doctors never could explain why Carol was born with only one arm," Inez Johnston said. "But it really didn't ever stop her. She handled it pretty well. She's a worker. She plugs away at things and doesn't give up."

Carol took piano lessons when she was young and at the age of 10 she began figure skating. Her mother had often taken her skating and Carol wanted to enter competition.

In two years, Carol had become very good. She won some local contests.

"Figure skating was very hard," Carol said. "You had to be very strong to push yourself

Carol's mother helps her put on her figure skates at the local community skating rink.

around the rink when you did a figure eight. And I weighed less than 50 pounds."

Inez Johnston remembers Carol tried almost anything when she was growing up.

"She tried everything the other kids did. When she learned to ride her sister's bicycle, we bought one for her. We tried not to be too protective. We felt she had to grow up. There are a lot of kids worse off than that," Carol's mother said.

In skating Carol was good at freestyle, which is doing what you want. And the music she had practiced at the piano helped her on the ice when she was skating.

Not long after Carol (on the right) started figure skating she won third place in a local skating competition.

When she was 12, Carol tried gymnastics and liked it. She was still able to use the music as she did in skating.

"We thought the gymnastics might be too difficult for Carol," said her mother. "It's so hard to do when you don't have two hands. But Carol was always so determined."

Years later, Mr. and Mrs. Johnston saw their youngest daughter compete in Seattle when she was an All-American. "We were very proud and thrilled," said Inez Johnston.

After Carol retired, she continued her education at Cal State-Fullerton. She coached

In Seattle Carol scored a 9.5 on the balance beam. A perfect score is 10.

young girls. She helped coach Rogers' program in many different ways.

"She's awesome," coach Rogers said. "She has a lot of class. Anytime she walks into the gym or anyplace, everyone knows she's there. Her chin is always up and her eyes are bright. She's a very special girl."

Carol has inspired people all over the country. She has appeared on many television shows to tell her story.

At the Hawaii Invitations in 1976 Carol came in first in the floor exercises.

"The most important thing in life is not to put yourself in a box," Carol said. "Don't ever say I can't do it. Just go out and have fun, that's how I started in gymnastics and skating.

"Kids should not be pushed into something they don't want to do. But they should be allowed to try what they want."

CHRONOLOGY

1958—Carol is born in Calgary, Canada, on March 10.

1968—Carol begins figure skating.

1970—Carol begins competing in gymnastics.

1976—Carol represents Canada in the Junior Olympics at Montreal.
 —She enrolls at Cal State-Fullerton.

1978—Carol wins the conference balance beam championship. She finishes third in floor exercise at the conference meet.

1978—Carol finishes second in the nation in both balance beam and floor exercise.
 —Carol is named All-American gymnast.

1979—Carol injures her knee and misses the season.
 —She begins filming the movie, "Lefty."

1980—Carol injures her knee again and retires from gymnastics.

1981—Carol graduates from Cal State-Fullerton. She enrolls in the Master's Program.

ABOUT THE AUTHOR

Pete Donovan, a native of New York, has been writing since he was 14. He is currently on the staff of the *Los Angeles Times,* where he covers a variety of sporting events, including professional baseball, college football, basketball, gymnastics, and tennis. He formerly worked as a marketing vice president for Jerry Buss's Los Angeles Strings. He is a founder of the Orange County Sportswriters Association and is the chief operating officer for the Orange County Sports Hall of Fame. Donovan also teaches a class at Cal State-Fullerton. He has covered Fullerton events for the past five years and has seen several of Carol Johnston's remarkable performances.